Xtreme Sports

Snowboarding

Aaron Carr

AV2

www.av2books.com

Step 1
Go to **www.av2books.com**

Step 2
Enter this unique code

Step 3
Explore your interactive eBook!

AV2 is optimized for use on any device

Your interactive eBook comes with...

- Read — **Audio** Listen to the entire book read aloud
- **Videos** Watch informative video clips
- **Weblinks** Gain additional information for research
- **Try This!** Complete activities and hands-on experiments
- **Key Words** Study vocabulary, and complete a matching word activity
- **Quizzes** Test your knowledge
- **Slideshows** View images and captions

View new titles and product videos at www.av2books.com

Xtreme Sports

Snowboarding

Contents

Snowboarding is a winter sport. Some people use snowboards to go down snowy mountains. Others do jumps and tricks.

Snowboards are long, flat boards with straps to hold people in place.

Pro snowboarders use many kinds of snowboards.

Snowboarders should always wear a helmet. Helmets keep snowboarders safe when they fall.

Pro snowboarders wear helmets and gloves.

People ride snowboards on hills and mountains covered with snow. Some snowboarders like to ride down steep hills.

Pro snowboarders learn to ride on many kinds of hills.

Practice is important for people who want to be good snowboarders.

Pro snowboarders practice for many hours every day.

People ride snowboards through a park doing jumps and tricks. This is called Slopestyle.

Pro snowboarders try to do hard tricks to get points.

Snowboarders fly off a big jump and do a trick in the air. This is called Big Air.

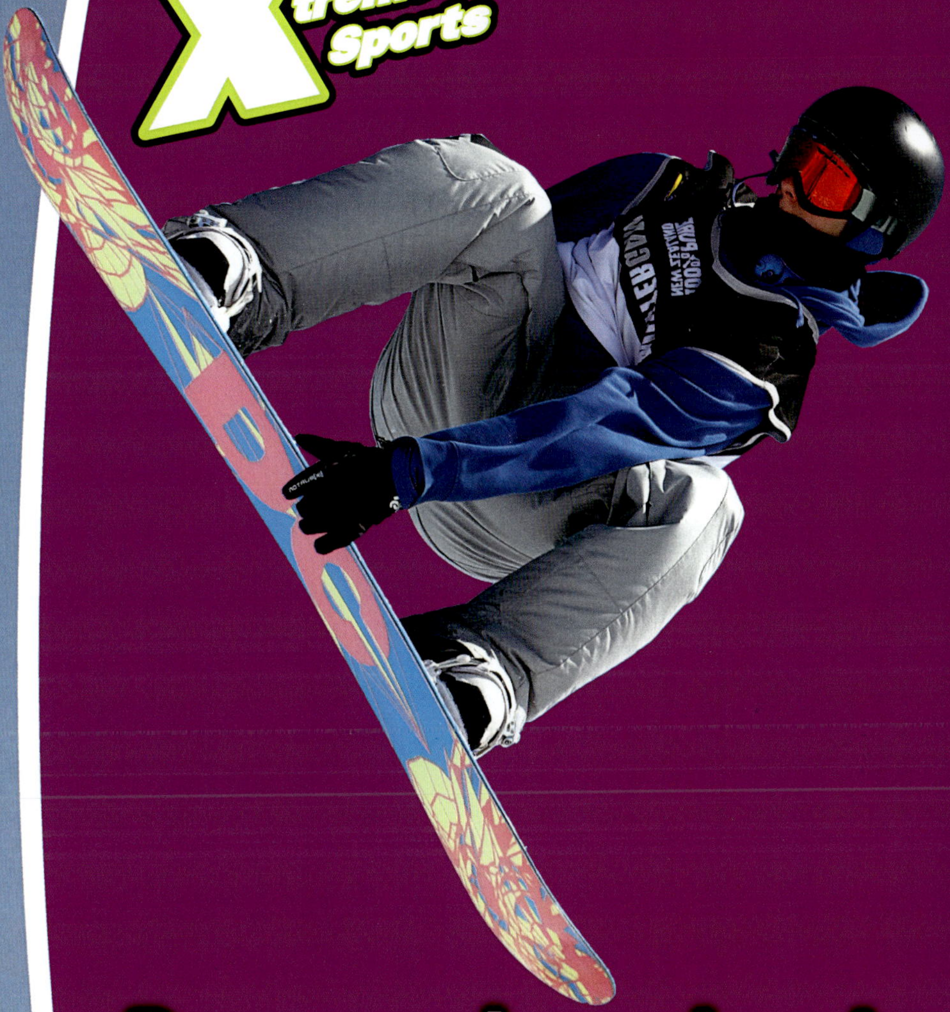

Pro snowboarders have to land after their trick.

Snowboarders ride down a hill, jumping off a U-shaped ramp. This is called Superpipe.

Pro snowboarders ride off the ramps to do big tricks in Superpipe.

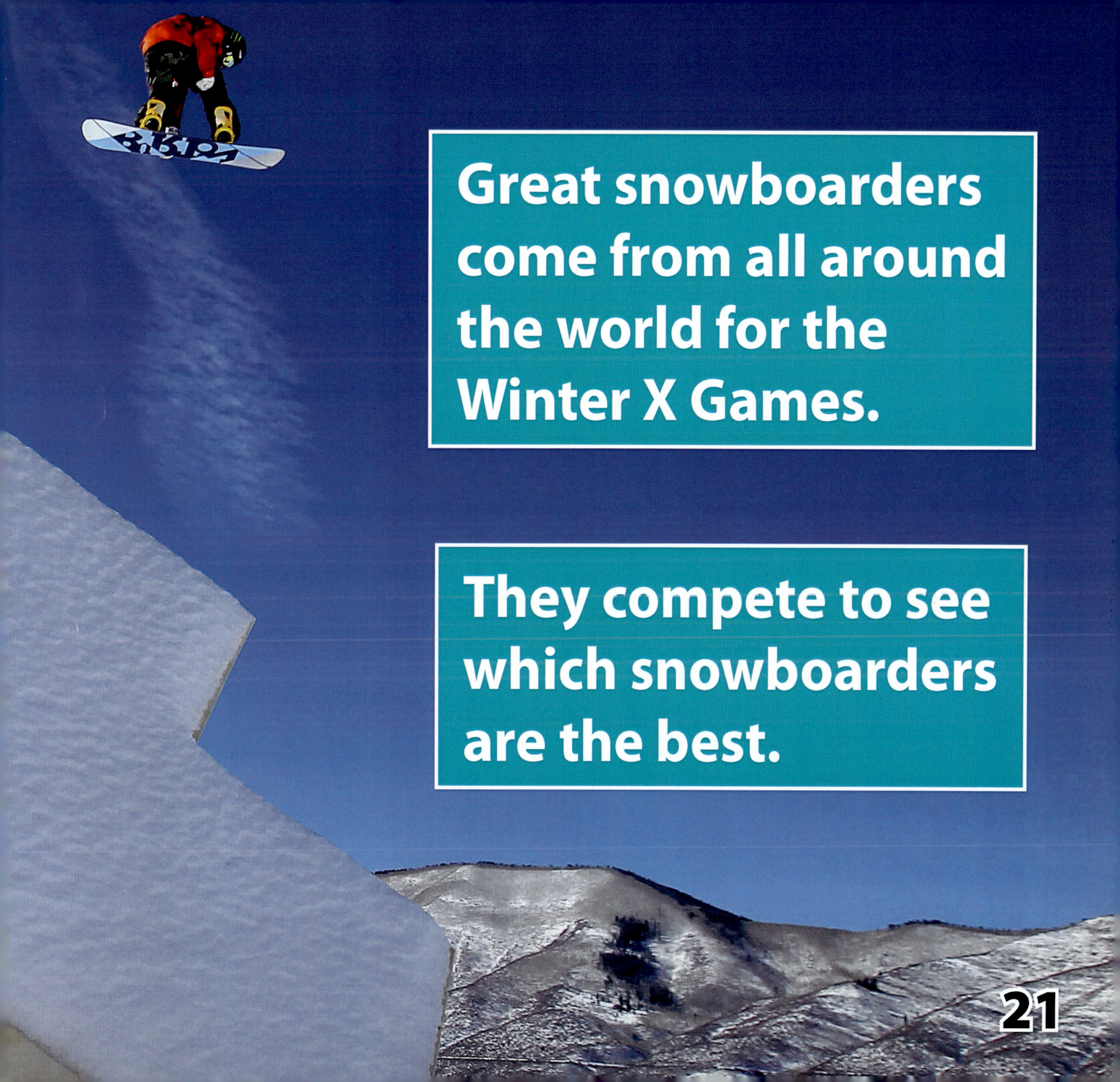

Great snowboarders come from all around the world for the Winter X Games.

They compete to see which snowboarders are the best.

SNOWBOARDING FACTS

These pages provide detailed information that expands on the interesting facts found in this book. These pages are intended to be used by adults as a learning support to help young readers round out their knowledge of each sport in the *Extreme Sports* series.

Pages 4–5

Snowboarding is one of the world's most popular winter sports. Snowboarders stand on a long board and ride it down snow-covered hills. They can perform a variety of tricks on the ground, in the air, and on rails and ledges. Snowboarders can also race down hills at high speeds. Snowboarding became popular in the 1990s, but it has been around since the 1960s.

Pages 6–7

Snowboards are made from many layers of materials, including wood, fiberglass, foam, and plastic. The edges are made of steel. This gives the snowboard better grip for turning. Snowboards have adjustable bindings to hold the snowboarder's feet in place. Sherman Poppen built the first snowboard in 1965 by strapping two skis together. He called it a "snurfer" because it surfed on snow.

Pages 8–9

The helmet is the most important piece of safety equipment. When falling down, a snowboarder's head may hit the ground. Helmets have saved many snowboarders from serious head injuries. Protection from the cold winter weather is also important. Many snowboarders wear snow pants, winter jackets, gloves, goggles, knee pads, and elbow pads.

Pages 10–11

Anyone with access to a snow-covered hill or mountain can snowboard. Boarders who like to ride fast will prefer the steep, smooth slopes found on ski hills. For snowboarders who want to perform tricks, most ski hills offer snowboard parks. These are enclosed areas with many obstacles that can be used to perform aerial stunts and tricks. Some ramps can be up to 130 feet (40 meters) high.

Pages 12–13

Practice is the most important part of becoming good at any sport, including snowboarding. Most professional snowboarders spend the winter practicing their moves on ski hills and in snowboard parks. They experiment with new tricks, obstacles, and terrain. Snowboarders improve their skills by learning new tricks while trying to master the moves they already know.

Pages 14–15

Slopestyle is a type of snowboarding that showcases the individual talent and style of each boarder. It takes place in a snowboard park that is mapped out like a course. Riders can choose their own route through the course, performing stunts and tricks on the obstacles that they choose. Boarders are judged on the style, variety, and difficulty of the tricks they perform.

Pages 16–17

Big Air is all about snowboarders showing off one amazing trick. Snowboarders get six runs and are judged based on all six of their runs. They will usually do a different trick on each run in order to show off to the judges. Judges look at the quality and difficulty of each trick, as well as how well snowboarders land after doing their tricks.

Pages 18–19

The Superpipe event takes place in a halfpipe. This is a 400-foot (122-m) long U-shaped channel with 15-foot (4.6-m) high ramps on each side. Boarders ride down one ramp before launching into the air off the opposite ramp. While in the air, boarders perform aerial stunts before landing. Riders continue doing tricks through the course. They earn points for the style, variety, difficulty, and height of their tricks.

Pages 20–21

The Winter X Games is an annual sports tournament that showcases the best athletes in extreme sports. The Winter X Games started in 1997. It includes events for snowboarding, skiing, and snowmobiling. These games attract the best extreme athletes from around the world each year. Some events feature athletes traveling down hills at high speeds and flying off ramps and into the air.

KEY WORDS

Research has shown that as much as 65 percent of all written material published in English is made up of 300 words. These 300 words cannot be taught using pictures or learned by sounding them out. They must be recognized by sight. This book contains 57 common sight words to help young readers improve their reading fluency and comprehension. This book also teaches young readers several important content words, such as proper nouns. These words are paired with pictures to aid in learning and improve understanding.

Page	Sight Words First Appearance
4	a, and, do, down, go, is, others, people, some, to, use
6	are, in, long, place, with
7	kinds, many, of
8	always, keep, should, they, when
10	like, on
11	learn
12	be, for, good, important, want, who
13	day, every
14	this, through
15	get, hard, points, try
16	air, big, off, the
17	after, have, land, their
21	all, around, come, from, great, see, which, world

Page	Content Words First Appearance
4	jumps, mountains, snowboarding, snowboards, sport, tricks
6	boards, straps
7	pro, snowboarders
8	helmet
9	gloves
10	hills, snow
12	practice
13	hours
14	park, Slopestyle
16	Big Air
18	ramp, Superpipe
21	Winter X Games

Published by AV2
14 Penn Plaza, 9th Floor New York, NY 10122
Website: www.av2books.com

Library of Congress Control Number: 2020935000

ISBN 978-1-7911-2696-4 (hardcover)
ISBN 978-1-7911-2697-1 (softcover)
ISBN 978-1-7911-2698-8 (multi-user eBook)
ISBN 978-1-7911-2699-5 (single-user eBook)

Printed in North Manchester, Indiana, United States of America
2 3 4 5 6 7 8 9 0 25 24 23 22 21

122021
131221

Art Director: Terry Paulhus Project Coordinator: Ryan Smith

Every reasonable effort has been made to trace ownership and to obtain permission to reprint copyright material. The publisher would be pleased to have any errors or omissions brought to its attention so that they may be corrected in subsequent printings.

The publisher acknowledges Getty Images, iStock, and Shutterstock as the primary image suppliers for this title.